Sound Design Mastery with FL Studio: Crafting Professional Sounds

Dive into synthesis, sampling, and FX chain techniques with detailed instructions and hands-on projects. This comprehensive resource equips you with the skills and knowledge to transform your sound design, making it perfect for music production, film scoring, and game audio. Unlock the full potential of FL Studio and take your sound design to the next level.

Table of Contents

Introduction

- Welcome to Sound Design Mastery
- The Art of Sound Design
- Why FL Studio?
- What You Will Learn
- How to Use This Book
- A Journey of Sonic Exploration

Chapter 1: Understanding Sound Design

- What is Sound Design?
- The Role of Sound Design in Music Production
- The Role of Sound Design in Other Media
- The Role of FL Studio in Sound Design
- The Importance of Sound Design
- Getting Started with Sound Design
- Sound Design Workflow
- Conclusion

Chapter 2: Synthesis Techniques with FL Studio

- Introduction to Synthesis
- Types of Synthesis

- Subtractive Synthesis
- FM Synthesis
- Additive Synthesis
- Wavetable Synthesis
- Granular Synthesis

- Built-In Synthesizers

  - Sytrus
  - Harmor
  - 3xOSC
  - Poizone
  - Toxic Biohazard

- Third-Party VST Synthesizers

  - Serum (Xfer Records)
  - Massive (Native Instruments)
  - Omnisphere (Spectrasonics)

- Practical Synthesis Examples
- Tips for Effective Synthesis
- Conclusion

Chapter 3: Sampling Strategies

- Introduction to Sampling
- The Basics of Sampling
- Tools for Sampling in FL Studio

- Edison
- DirectWave
- FPC (Fruity Pad Controller)
- Slicex

- Sampling Techniques

  - Field Recording
  - Resampling
  - Creative Sampling

- Practical Sampling Examples
- Tips for Effective Sampling
- Conclusion

Chapter 4: FX Chain Exploration

- Introduction to FX Chains
- Understanding Signal Processing
- Built-In Effects in FL Studio

  - EQ (Parametric EQ 2)
  - Reverb (Fruity Reeverb 2)
  - Delay (Fruity Delay 3)
  - Compression (Fruity Limiter)
  - Distortion (Fruity Fast Dist)

- Third-Party VST Effects

- FabFilter Pro-Q 3
- Valhalla Room
- Soundtoys EchoBoy

- FX Chain Techniques

  - Signal Routing
  - Creative Processing
  - Parallel Processing

- Practical FX Chain Examples
- Tips for Effective FX Chains
- Conclusion

Chapter 5: Advanced Sound Design Techniques

- Introduction
- Layering Sounds

  - Basics of Layering
  - Practical Layering Examples

- Modulation and Automation

  - Modulation
  - Practical Modulation Examples

- Sound Design for Different Genres

- Electronic Music
- Hip Hop and Trap
- Film Scoring and Sound Effects

- Practical Advanced Techniques Examples
- Tips for Advanced Sound Design
- Conclusion

Chapter 6: Practical Sound Design Projects

- Introduction
- Project 1: Creating a Signature Bass Sound
- Project 2: Crafting a Unique Drum Kit
- Project 3: Designing a Cinematic Soundscape
- Project 4: Building an Evolving Lead Sound
- Project 5: Crafting a Glitch Effect
- Tips for Successful Sound Design Projects
- Conclusion

Chapter 7: Troubleshooting and Tips

- Introduction
- Common Sound Design Issues
    - Muddy Mixes
    - Weak Sounds
    - Harsh Frequencies

- Workflow Tips

    - Organizing Your Project
    - Efficient Sound Design
    - Backup and Version Control

- Creative Tips

    - Breaking Creative Blocks
    - Experimentation
    - Collaborating with Others

- Conclusion

Conclusion

- The Journey of Sound Design Mastery
- Key Takeaways
- The Path Forward
- Final Thoughts

Index

Introduction

Welcome to "Sound Design Mastery with FL Studio: Crafting Professional Sounds." This book is your ultimate guide to the world of sound design, tailored specifically for FL Studio users. Whether you're a beginner stepping into the realm of audio production or an experienced producer looking to refine your skills, this book provides you with the knowledge, techniques, and practical insights needed to create distinctive and professional sounds.

The Art of Sound Design

Sound design is more than just creating pleasant sounds; it's about sculpting audio to evoke emotions, tell stories, and enhance experiences. From the pulsating basslines of electronic music to the eerie atmospheres in film, sound design plays a crucial role in various media. As a sound designer, you have the power to shape the auditory landscape and influence how listeners perceive and interact with sound.

Why FL Studio?

FL Studio, developed by Image-Line, is a powerful and versatile Digital Audio Workstation (DAW) that has become a favorite among producers and sound designers worldwide. Its intuitive interface, robust set of built-in tools, and extensive compatibility with third-party plugins make it an ideal platform for sound design. FL Studio offers a rich playground for creativity, allowing you to experiment, innovate, and bring your sonic ideas to life.

What You Will Learn

This book is structured to provide a comprehensive understanding of sound design using FL Studio. Here's a brief overview of what you can expect:

1. **Synthesis Techniques** : Dive deep into the art of synthesis using FL Studio's powerful built-in synthesizers and popular third-party VSTs. Learn how to create everything from basic tones to complex textures using subtractive, FM, additive, wavetable, and granular synthesis techniques.
2. **Sampling Strategies** : Discover the world of sampling and learn how to capture, edit, and manipulate audio to create unique sounds. We'll explore FL Studio's sampling tools like Edison, DirectWave, FPC, and Slicex, providing practical examples and advanced techniques.
3. **FX Chain Creation** : Explore the vast array of built-in effects in FL Studio and learn how to create intricate FX chains that enhance your sounds. From EQ and reverb to delay and distortion, we'll cover essential signal processing and creative effects techniques.
4. **Advanced Sound Design Techniques** : Go beyond the basics and delve into advanced sound design methods. Learn how to layer sounds, use modulation

and automation effectively, and design sounds for different genres and applications.
5. **Practical Sound Design Projects** : Apply your knowledge through hands-on projects that guide you step-by-step in creating signature sounds, custom drum kits, cinematic soundscapes, evolving lead sounds, and glitch effects.
6. **Troubleshooting and Tips** : Overcome common sound design challenges with practical tips and solutions. Improve your workflow, break through creative blocks, and discover strategies for efficient and innovative sound design.

How to Use This Book

This book is designed to be both instructional and inspirational. Each chapter builds upon the previous one, providing a structured learning path. However, feel free to jump to sections that interest you the most or that suit your current needs. Practical examples and exercises are included throughout the book to help you apply what you've learned and develop your skills hands-on.

A Journey of Sonic Exploration

Sound design is a journey of exploration and creativity. As you progress through this book, I encourage you to experiment, take risks, and push the boundaries of what's possible. FL Studio is a powerful tool, but the true magic comes from your imagination and innovation. Embrace the process, learn from

your mistakes, and enjoy the art of crafting professional sounds.
Welcome to the world of sound design with FL Studio. Let's get started and create something extraordinary together!

Chapter 1: Understanding Sound Design

What is Sound Design?

Sound design is the process of creating, manipulating, and combining audio elements to produce specific auditory effects or experiences. It is an essential aspect of various fields, including music production, film, video games, and virtual reality. Sound design can range from crafting the perfect synth lead for a song to creating the atmospheric sounds of a fantasy world in a video game.
Sound design encompasses a wide range of activities:

- **Creating original sounds from scratch using synthesis techniques**
- **Recording and editing real-world sounds through sampling**
- **Applying effects and processing to shape and enhance audio**

The Role of Sound Design in Music Production

In music production, sound design is crucial for defining the character and mood of a track. It can transform a simple melody into a powerful lead, give a bassline the depth and punch it needs, or create the intricate textures that make a piece of music stand out. Sound design helps producers craft unique sonic identities and ensures their music resonates with listeners.

The Role of Sound Design in Other Media

Beyond music, sound design plays a vital role in other media:

- **Film** : Enhances the emotional impact of scenes through Foley effects, ambient sounds, and music.
- **Video Games** : Creates immersive environments and provides audio feedback to player actions.
- **Virtual Reality (VR)** : Builds realistic and interactive soundscapes that enhance the sense of presence.

The Role of FL Studio in Sound Design

FL Studio is a versatile DAW that offers a comprehensive suite of tools for sound design. Its user-friendly interface, powerful built-in plugins, and compatibility with third-party VSTs make it an ideal platform for both beginners and experienced sound designers.

Key Features of FL Studio for Sound Design

- **Built-In Synthesizers** : FL Studio includes powerful synthesizers like Sytrus, Harmor, and 3xOSC, which are capable of creating a wide range of sounds.
- **Sampling Tools** : Tools like Edison, DirectWave, and Slicex provide robust capabilities for recording, editing, and manipulating audio samples.
- **Effects Processing** : A vast array of built-in effects, including EQs, reverbs, delays, and compressors, allow for detailed sound shaping and enhancement.
- **Automation and Modulation** : FL Studio's automation and modulation features enable dynamic changes and intricate sound movements.
- **User-Friendly Interface** : The intuitive layout and workflow of FL Studio make it accessible for users at all levels.

The Importance of Sound Design

Sound design is essential for creating engaging and memorable auditory experiences. In music, it can define a genre or artist's signature sound. In film and games, it enhances storytelling and immersion. Effective sound design can evoke emotions, build tension, create atmosphere, and provide critical feedback to users.

Examples of Impactful Sound Design

- **Music** : The distinct bass sound in dubstep tracks, the lush pads in ambient music, and the intricate leads in electronic dance music (EDM) all rely on sound design.
- **Film** : The iconic lightsaber sound in "Star Wars," the chilling footsteps in horror films, and the immersive ambiances in sci-fi movies showcase the power of sound design.
- **Games** : The realistic gunfire in first-person shooters, the magical spell effects in fantasy RPGs, and the ambient sounds in open-world games enhance the player's experience.

Getting Started with Sound Design

To begin your journey in sound design, you'll need to familiarize yourself with the basic concepts and tools. Here are some initial steps:

1. **Learn the Basics of Audio** : Understand fundamental concepts like frequency, amplitude, waveform, and envelope.
2. **Explore FL Studio** : Get comfortable with FL Studio's interface, navigation, and workflow.
3. **Experiment with Built-In Plugins** : Start by using FL Studio's built-in synthesizers and effects to create and manipulate sounds.
4. **Practice Regularly** : Consistent practice is key to mastering sound design. Experiment, make mistakes, and learn from them.

Sound Design Workflow

A typical sound design workflow in FL Studio might involve the following steps:

1. **Conceptualization** : Define the type of sound you want to create and its role in your project.
2. **Sound Creation** : Use synthesis or sampling to generate the initial sound.
3. **Processing** : Apply effects and processing to shape and enhance the sound.
4. **Layering** : Combine multiple sounds to create a richer and more complex final result.
5. **Fine-Tuning** : Adjust parameters, automate changes, and refine the sound.
6. **Integration** : Incorporate the sound into your project and ensure it fits well with other elements.

Conclusion

Understanding the fundamentals of sound design is the first step toward creating professional and distinctive sounds. With FL Studio, you have a powerful toolset at your disposal, allowing you to explore, experiment, and innovate. As you progress through this book, you'll gain the knowledge and skills needed to master sound design and bring your creative visions to life.

Chapter 2: Synthesis Techniques with FL Studio

Introduction to Synthesis

Synthesis is the art of generating sound using electronic devices. It is the foundation of sound design, allowing you to create everything from simple tones to complex, evolving textures. FL Studio provides a variety of built-in synthesizers, each with unique features and capabilities. In this chapter, we will explore the different types of synthesis and how to use FL Studio's synthesizers to create a wide range of sounds.

Types of Synthesis

1. **Subtractive Synthesis** : This technique starts with a rich, harmonically complex sound and shapes it by subtracting frequencies using filters. It's the basis of classic analog synth sounds.
2. **FM Synthesis** : Frequency Modulation (FM) synthesis generates complex waveforms by modulating the frequency of one oscillator with another. It can produce metallic and bell-like sounds, among other complex textures.
3. **Additive Synthesis** : This method builds sounds by adding together individual sine waves (harmonics). It's useful for creating complex, evolving sounds and precise control over the harmonic content.

4. **Wavetable Synthesis** : Wavetable synthesis involves cycling through different waveforms stored in a table, allowing for dynamic and evolving sounds.
5. **Granular Synthesis** : This advanced technique involves breaking down a sound into tiny grains and manipulating them to create textures and ambiences.

Built-In Synthesizers in FL Studio

Sytrus

Sytrus is a hybrid synthesizer that combines subtractive, FM, and additive synthesis. It is one of FL Studio's most versatile and powerful synthesizers.

- **Basic Operation** :

    - Navigate the interface to understand the various sections: Operators, Modulation Matrix, Filters, and Effects.
    - Load presets to get a feel for the range of sounds Sytrus can produce.
    - Create basic sounds by starting with simple waveforms and applying filters and effects.

- **Advanced Techniques** :

    - **Modulation** : Use the Modulation Matrix to create complex interactions between operators.

- **Waveform Shaping** : Customize the waveforms of each operator for unique timbres.
- **FM Synthesis** : Explore FM synthesis by modulating operators with each other.

Harmor

Harmor is an advanced additive/subtractive synthesizer with powerful resynthesis capabilities.

- **Basic Operation** :

    - Understand the interface, including the Harmonic and Image sections.
    - Load and modify presets to learn how Harmor's features work together.
    - Create basic sounds using the additive synthesis engine and built-in effects.

- **Advanced Techniques** :

    - **Image Resynthesis** : Import images or audio files and use Harmor to resynthesize them into playable sounds.
    - **Harmonic Unison** : Use unison settings to create thick, detuned sounds.
    - **Envelope Control** : Utilize Harmor's extensive envelope controls for dynamic sound shaping.

3xOSC

3xOSC is a simple yet effective subtractive synthesizer ideal for basic sound design tasks.

- **Basic Operation** :

  - Navigate the interface to understand the three oscillators and their controls.
  - Load presets to see how different settings affect the sound.
  - Create basic sounds by adjusting the waveforms, tuning, and mix levels of the oscillators.

- **Advanced Techniques** :

  - **Layering** : Combine multiple instances of 3xOSC to create richer sounds.
  - **Modulation** : Use automation and external modulation sources to add movement to your sounds.
  - **Effects Processing** : Enhance 3xOSC sounds with FL Studio's effects plugins.

Poizone

Poizone is a subtractive synthesizer with a simple interface but powerful sound-shaping capabilities.

- **Basic Operation** :

  - Familiarize yourself with the interface, focusing on the oscillators, filter, and modulation sections.
  - Load and tweak presets to understand how Poizone's features interact.
  - Create basic sounds by adjusting the oscillators and applying filters.

- **Advanced Techniques** :

  - **Modulation Matrix** : Use the modulation matrix to create dynamic changes in your sounds.
  - **Built-In Effects** : Apply Poizone's built-in effects to enhance your patches.
  - **Waveform Blending** : Blend different waveforms for unique timbres.

Toxic Biohazard

Toxic Biohazard is a hybrid FM/subtractive synthesizer with a distinctive sound.

- **Basic Operation** :

  - Explore the interface, focusing on the oscillators, FM matrix, and filters.
  - Load and experiment with presets to see how different settings affect the sound.

- Create basic sounds using the FM synthesis engine and subtractive filtering.

- **Advanced Techniques** :

  - **FM Matrix** : Utilize the FM matrix to create complex modulations between oscillators.
  - **Modulation and Effects** : Apply internal modulation sources and effects to enhance your sounds.
  - **Custom Waveforms** : Design custom waveforms for the oscillators to create unique timbres.

Third-Party VST Synthesizers

Serum (Xfer Records)

Serum is a wavetable synthesizer known for its high-quality sound and intuitive interface.

- **Basic Operation** :

  - Navigate the interface, focusing on the oscillators, filters, and effects sections.
  - Load and tweak presets to understand how Serum's features work together.
  - Create basic sounds by selecting wavetables and applying filters and effects.

- **Advanced Techniques** :

    - **Custom Wavetables** : Import and design your own wavetables for unique sounds.
    - **Modulation** : Use the extensive modulation options, including LFOs, envelopes, and macros.
    - **Effects Section** : Utilize Serum's built-in effects to enhance your patches.

Massive (Native Instruments)

Massive is a powerful wavetable synthesizer popular in electronic music production.

- **Basic Operation** :

    - Understand the interface, focusing on the oscillators, modulation, and effects sections.
    - Load and modify presets to learn how Massive's features interact.
    - Create basic sounds by selecting wavetables and applying filters and effects.

- **Advanced Techniques** :

    - **Modulation Matrix** : Use the modulation matrix to create dynamic changes in your sounds.
    - **Performer** : Utilize the performer section to add rhythmic modulation.

- **Macro Controls** : Assign parameters to macro controls for easy manipulation.

Omnisphere (Spectrasonics)

Omnisphere is a versatile synthesizer with a vast library of sounds and powerful synthesis capabilities.

- **Basic Operation** :

    - Explore the interface, focusing on the oscillators, filters, and modulation sections.
    - Load and experiment with patches to understand how Omnisphere's features work together.
    - Create basic sounds by selecting sound sources and applying synthesis techniques.

- **Advanced Techniques** :

    - **Synthesis Engines** : Use the various synthesis engines, including granular and wavetable synthesis.
    - **Sound Design Tools** : Utilize Omnisphere's extensive sound design tools, including modulation and effects.
    - **Layering and Stacking** : Combine multiple layers and sound sources for complex patches.

Practical Synthesis Examples

1. **Create a Basic Bass Sound** : Using Sytrus, design a deep, punchy bass.

    - **Step-by-Step** : Start with a sine wave, apply a low-pass filter, add distortion and compression for punch.

2. **Design a Lead Synth** : Use Harmor to create a soaring lead sound.

    - **Step-by-Step** : Select a saw wave, apply unison for detuning, add reverb and delay for space.

3. **Build a Pad Sound** : Craft a lush pad using 3xOSC.

    - **Step-by-Step** : Layer oscillators with different waveforms, apply a slow attack and release, add chorus and reverb.

4. **Make a Wavetable Sweep** : Create a dynamic wavetable sweep with Serum.

    - **Step-by-Step** : Choose a wavetable, automate the wavetable position, add filter sweeps and effects.

5. **Create a Granular Texture** : Use Harmor's resynthesis capabilities to create a granular texture.

    - **Step-by-Step** : Import a sample, apply granular synthesis, modulate parameters for evolving texture.

Tips for Effective Synthesis

1. **Understand the Basics** : Master the fundamental concepts of synthesis before diving into complex techniques.
2. **Experiment** : Don't be afraid to try different settings and combinations to discover unique sounds.
3. **Use Modulation** : Modulation adds movement and interest to your sounds; explore LFOs, envelopes, and automation.
4. **Layer Sounds** : Combining multiple layers can create richer, more complex sounds.
5. **Save Your Patches** : Save your favorite patches and settings for future use and inspiration.

Conclusion

Mastering synthesis is a journey that requires practice and experimentation. FL Studio's powerful built-in synthesizers and third-party VSTs provide a rich toolkit for sound design. By understanding the different types of synthesis and how to apply them, you'll be able to create a wide range of professional and distinctive sounds. As you progress through this book, you'll continue to build on these foundational skills, exploring more advanced techniques and creative possibilities in sound design.

Chapter 3: Sampling Strategies

Introduction to Sampling

Sampling involves recording, editing, and manipulating audio snippets to create new sounds. It is a fundamental aspect of sound design, allowing you to capture real-world sounds and integrate them into your projects. FL Studio offers a range of powerful tools for sampling, making it easy to capture, edit, and use samples creatively.

The Basics of Sampling

Sampling can be broken down into several key steps:

1. **Recording** : Capturing audio from various sources.
2. **Editing** : Trimming, looping, and adjusting the recorded audio.
3. **Processing** : Applying effects and manipulations to the sample.
4. **Integration** : Using the sample in your project, often as part of a larger composition.

Tools for Sampling in FL Studio

Edison

Edison is a versatile audio editor and recorder built into FL Studio. It provides a comprehensive set of tools for recording, editing, and processing samples.

- **Basic Operation** :

    - **Recording** : Open Edison in an effect slot on any channel, and press the record button to start capturing audio.
    - **Editing** : Use the selection tools to trim, cut, copy, and paste audio. Apply fades, normalize, and reverse audio clips.
    - **Saving** : Save your edited samples directly from Edison for use in your projects.

- **Advanced Techniques** :

    - **Noise Reduction** : Use the noise reduction tool to clean up recordings.
    - **Time-Stretching** : Change the length of a sample without affecting its pitch.
    - **Pitch-Shifting** : Alter the pitch of a sample without changing its duration.

DirectWave

DirectWave is a powerful sampler capable of importing and manipulating multisamples. It allows for detailed control over sample playback and manipulation.

- **Basic Operation** :

  - **Loading Samples** : Import samples or multisample libraries into DirectWave.
  - **Mapping Zones** : Assign samples to different keys or velocity ranges for detailed control.
  - **Basic Playback** : Adjust playback parameters like pitch, volume, and panning.

- **Advanced Techniques** :

  - **Velocity Layering** : Create dynamic instruments by layering samples triggered at different velocities.
  - **Round-Robin Sampling** : Alternate between different samples to avoid the repetitive sound of single-sample triggering.
  - **Modulation** : Use LFOs and envelopes to modulate various sample parameters.

FPC (Fruity Pad Controller)

FPC is a drum sampler designed for creating custom drum kits and percussive sounds. It allows you to map samples to pads, making it ideal for beat-making.

- **Basic Operation** :

    - **Loading Samples** : Import samples into FPC and assign them to pads.
    - **Basic Controls** : Adjust volume, pitch, and panning for each pad.
    - **Creating Kits** : Save custom drum kits for use in your projects.

- **Advanced Techniques** :

    - **Layering Sounds** : Assign multiple samples to a single pad for layered drum hits.
    - **Velocity Sensitivity** : Set velocity layers to create dynamic drum sounds.
    - **MIDI Mapping** : Map pads to external MIDI controllers for real-time performance.

Slicex

Slicex is a powerful tool for slicing and manipulating loops. It automatically detects transients and slices loops into individual segments that can be triggered and rearranged.

- **Basic Operation** :

  - **Loading Loops** : Import loops into Slicex for automatic slicing.
  - **Slicing Controls** : Adjust the sensitivity of transient detection and manually add or remove slices.
  - **Basic Playback** : Trigger individual slices using MIDI or the built-in keyboard.

- **Advanced Techniques** :

  - **Time-Stretching Slices** : Stretch individual slices without affecting their pitch.
  - **Pitch-Shifting Slices** : Change the pitch of slices independently of their duration.
  - **Effects Processing** : Apply effects to individual slices or the entire loop for creative manipulation.

Sampling Techniques

Field Recording

Field recording involves capturing sounds from the environment using portable recording equipment. These recordings can add a unique and organic element to your projects.

- **Equipment** : Use portable recorders or smartphones to capture audio.
- **Recording Tips** : Focus on interesting sounds, minimize background noise, and experiment with different environments.
- **Applications** : Use field recordings to create ambient soundscapes, Foley effects, or as the basis for unique samples.

Resampling

Resampling involves recording the output of your DAW or a specific instrument and then manipulating the recorded audio. This technique allows for complex sound design and layering.

- **Basic Technique** : Route the output of a channel to a recording input and capture the audio.
- **Creative Applications** : Apply effects to the resampled audio, reverse it, or layer it with the original sound for unique textures.

Creative Sampling

Creative sampling involves using unconventional sources and techniques to generate unique sounds. This can include anything from sampling household objects to manipulating found sounds.

- **Unconventional Sources** : Record and sample sounds from everyday objects, like kitchen utensils, paper, or toys.
- **Manipulation Techniques** : Use extreme pitch-shifting, time-stretching, and effects processing to transform ordinary sounds into extraordinary ones.
- **Applications** : Create percussion sounds, ambient textures, or unique sound effects.

Practical Sampling Examples

1. **Record and Edit a Sample with Edison** :

    - **Step-by-Step** : Open Edison, record an audio source, trim and edit the sample, and save it for use in your project.

2. **Create a Drum Kit with FPC** :

    - **Step-by-Step** : Load various drum samples into FPC, assign them to pads, and adjust parameters like volume and pitch to create a cohesive kit.

3. **Resample and Transform Audio with DirectWave** :

    - **Step-by-Step** : Record a synth patch, import the recording into DirectWave, apply modulation and effects, and use the transformed sound in your project.

4. **Slice and Rearrange a Loop with Slicex** :

    - **Step-by-Step** : Import a drum loop into Slicex, adjust slice points, rearrange slices to create a new pattern, and apply effects to individual slices.

5. **Field Recording Adventure** :

    - **Step-by-Step** : Capture environmental sounds, edit and clean the recordings, and integrate them into a soundscape or as elements in a track.

Tips for Effective Sampling

1. **Capture High-Quality Audio** : Use good recording equipment and techniques to ensure clean, high-quality samples.
2. **Organize Your Samples** : Keep your samples organized in folders with clear names for easy access.
3. **Experiment with Effects** : Use effects like reverb, delay, and distortion to creatively manipulate your samples.
4. **Use Layering** : Combine multiple samples to create rich, complex sounds.
5. **Be Creative** : Don't be afraid to experiment with unconventional sources and techniques.

Conclusion

Sampling is a powerful tool in sound design, allowing you to capture and manipulate audio to create unique sounds. FL Studio's robust sampling tools, such as Edison, DirectWave, FPC, and Slicex, provide a wide range of options for recording, editing, and transforming samples. By mastering these tools and techniques, you'll be able to add a new dimension to your sound design projects, making your music and audio productions stand out. As you continue through this book, you'll build on these foundational skills, exploring more advanced techniques and creative possibilities in sound design.

Chapter 4: FX Chain Exploration

Introduction to FX Chains

An FX chain is a series of audio effects applied to a sound to shape its character. Effects processing is a crucial part of sound design, allowing you to enhance, transform, and manipulate sounds in creative ways. FL Studio offers a vast array of built-in effects, from EQ and compression to reverb and delay, as well as compatibility with third-party VST plugins.

Understanding Signal Processing

Signal processing involves manipulating audio signals using various effects to achieve the desired sound. Common signal processing effects include:

1. **Equalization (EQ)** : Adjusts the balance of different frequency components in a sound.
2. **Compression** : Controls the dynamic range of a sound by reducing the volume of loud parts and boosting quiet parts.
3. **Reverb** : Adds a sense of space and depth to a sound, simulating different acoustic environments.
4. **Delay** : Creates echoes and rhythmic patterns by repeating the sound at set intervals.
5. **Distortion** : Adds harmonic overtones to a sound, making it grittier and more aggressive.

Built-In Effects in FL Studio

EQ (Parametric EQ 2)

Parametric EQ 2 is a versatile equalizer for shaping the tonal balance of your sounds.

- **Basic Operation** :

- **Bands** : Adjust up to seven frequency bands with precise control over gain, frequency, and bandwidth.
- **Visualization** : Use the real-time spectrum analyzer to visualize the frequency content of your sound.
- **Presets** : Start with presets to quickly apply common EQ settings.

- **Advanced Techniques** :

  - **Dynamic EQ** : Use automation to dynamically adjust EQ settings over time.
  - **Mid/Side Processing** : Separate and process the mid and side components of a stereo signal independently.
  - **Harmonic Enhancement** : Boost or cut specific harmonics to enhance the tonal characteristics of your sound.

Reverb (Fruity Reeverb 2)

Fruity Reeverb 2 adds space and depth to your sounds with reverb.

- **Basic Operation** :

  - **Pre-Delay** : Set the time before the reverb effect begins.
  - **Decay** : Control how long the reverb tail lasts.

- **Damping** : Adjust the absorption of high frequencies to simulate different materials.

- **Advanced Techniques** :

  - **Lush Reverbs** : Create rich, ambient spaces with long decay times and moderate damping.
  - **Realistic Environments** : Simulate realistic acoustic spaces by fine-tuning pre-delay, decay, and damping.
  - **Creative Reverbs** : Use extreme settings for creative effects, such as reverse reverb or gated reverb.

Delay (Fruity Delay 3)

Fruity Delay 3 adds echoes and rhythmic patterns with delay.

- **Basic Operation** :

  - **Time** : Set the delay time in milliseconds or sync it to the project tempo.
  - **Feedback** : Control how many times the delay repeats.
  - **Mix** : Adjust the balance between the dry and wet signals.

- **Advanced Techniques** :

- **Ping-Pong Delay** : Create stereo effects by alternating the delay between the left and right channels.
- **Tempo-Synced Delays** : Sync the delay time to your project's tempo for rhythmic effects.
- **Creative Modulation** : Use modulation to vary the delay time and feedback for evolving effects.

Compression (Fruity Limiter)

Fruity Limiter controls dynamics and adds punch with compression.

- **Basic Operation** :

  - **Threshold** : Set the level at which compression begins.
  - **Ratio** : Determine how much compression is applied once the threshold is exceeded.
  - **Attack and Release** : Control how quickly the compressor responds to changes in the signal level.

- **Advanced Techniques** :

  - **Sidechain Compression** : Duck one sound in response to another, commonly used in electronic music.
  - **Parallel Compression** : Blend compressed and uncompressed signals for a more natural sound.

- **Multiband Compression** : Apply compression to different frequency bands independently.

Distortion (Fruity Fast Dist)

Fruity Fast Dist adds grit and character with distortion.

- **Basic Operation** :

    - **Drive** : Control the amount of distortion applied to the signal.
    - **Tone** : Adjust the frequency balance of the distorted signal.
    - **Mix** : Blend the distorted signal with the original sound.

- **Advanced Techniques** :

    - **Different Distortion Types** : Experiment with different distortion types, such as overdrive, fuzz, and bitcrushing.
    - **Parallel Distortion** : Blend distorted and clean signals for added complexity.
    - **Distortion as a Creative Tool** : Use distortion creatively to transform sounds and create unique textures.

Third-Party VST Effects

FabFilter Pro-Q 3

FabFilter Pro-Q 3 is a highly versatile EQ with advanced features.

- **Basic Operation** :

    - **Bands** : Adjust multiple frequency bands with precise control.
    - **Dynamic EQ** : Use dynamic EQ to respond to changes in the signal level.
    - **Visualization** : Real-time spectrum analyzer for visual feedback.

- **Advanced Techniques** :

    - **Linear Phase Mode** : Use linear phase mode for transparent EQ adjustments.
    - **Mid/Side Processing** : Separate and process mid and side components independently.
    - **Notch Filters** : Apply notch filters to remove specific frequencies.

Valhalla Room

Valhalla Room is a high-quality reverb plugin known for its lush sound.

- **Basic Operation** :

    - **Pre-Delay** : Set the time before the reverb effect begins.
    - **Decay** : Control the length of the reverb tail.
    - **Mix** : Adjust the balance between the dry and wet signals.

- **Advanced Techniques** :

    - **Ambience Creation** : Use Valhalla Room to create ambient soundscapes with long decay times.
    - **Realistic Spaces** : Simulate realistic acoustic environments with precise control over reverb parameters.
    - **Modulation** : Use modulation to add subtle movement to the reverb tail.

Soundtoys EchoBoy

Soundtoys EchoBoy is a versatile delay plugin with a wide range of delay types and styles.

- **Basic Operation** :

    - **Delay Time** : Set the delay time in milliseconds or sync it to the project tempo.
    - **Feedback** : Control the number of repeats.
    - **Mix** : Adjust the balance between the dry and wet signals.

- **Advanced Techniques** :

    - **Tape Echo Emulation** : Use EchoBoy's tape echo emulation for vintage delay sounds.
    - **Rhythmic Delays** : Sync the delay time to your project's tempo for rhythmic effects.
    - **Creative Modulation** : Use modulation to vary the delay time and feedback for evolving effects.

FX Chain Techniques

Signal Routing

Signal routing involves directing audio through various channels and effects to achieve complex processing.

- **Basic Routing** : Route audio through multiple effects in series for layered processing.
- **Parallel Processing** : Split the signal into multiple paths, process each path differently, and then combine them.

- **Send Effects** : Use send channels to apply effects to multiple tracks simultaneously.

Creative Processing

Creative processing involves using effects in unconventional ways to achieve unique sounds.

- **Unconventional Combinations** : Experiment with unusual combinations of effects.
- **Extreme Settings** : Use extreme effect settings for dramatic transformations.
- **Automation** : Automate effect parameters to add movement and variation.

Parallel Processing

Parallel processing involves splitting the signal and processing each split separately.

- **Basic Technique** : Duplicate the signal, apply different effects to each copy, and blend them together.
- **Applications** : Enhance depth, clarity, and impact by combining processed and unprocessed signals.
- **Examples** : Parallel compression, parallel distortion, and parallel EQ.

Practical FX Chain Examples

1. **Build an FX Chain for a Lead Sound** :

    - **Step-by-Step** : Use EQ to shape the tone, compression to add punch, reverb for space, and delay for movement.

2. **Create a Reverb Space** :

    - **Step-by-Step** : Use Fruity Reeverb 2 to design a unique reverb environment with pre-delay, decay, and damping.

3. **Experiment with Delay** :

    - **Step-by-Step** : Apply Fruity Delay 3 creatively to a vocal sample, using ping-pong delay and tempo-synced effects.

4. **Distort and Destroy** :

    - **Step-by-Step** : Use Fruity Fast Dist to add grit and character to a bass sound, blending the distorted signal with the clean sound.

5. **Dynamic EQ** :

- **Step-by-Step** : Use FabFilter Pro-Q 3 to control problem frequencies dynamically, applying EQ changes only when needed.

Tips for Effective FX Chains

1. **Start Simple** : Begin with basic effects and gradually add more complex processing as needed.
2. **Experiment** : Don't be afraid to try unconventional effect combinations and settings.
3. **Use Automation** : Automate effect parameters to add movement and variation.
4. **Layer Effects** : Combine multiple effects to create rich, complex sounds.
5. **Save Presets** : Save your favorite FX chain settings as presets for easy recall.

Conclusion

Exploring FX chains and effects processing is a vital aspect of sound design, allowing you to shape and enhance your sounds in creative ways. FL Studio's built-in effects and third-party VST plugins provide a wide range of options for signal processing. By mastering these tools and techniques, you'll be able to create professional and distinctive sounds that stand out in your music and audio productions. As you continue through this book, you'll build on these foundational skills, exploring more advanced techniques and creative possibilities in sound design.

Chapter 5: Advanced Sound Design Techniques

Introduction

As you progress in your sound design journey, you'll need to employ advanced techniques to create more intricate and unique sounds. This chapter delves into layering, modulation, automation, and genre-specific sound design strategies to help you push the boundaries of your creativity.

Layering Sounds

Layering involves combining multiple sounds to create a richer, more complex result. It's a fundamental technique in sound design that can add depth and texture to your sounds.

Basics of Layering

1. **Choose Complementary Sounds** : Select sounds that complement each other in terms of frequency, texture, and character.
2. **Frequency Ranges** : Ensure that each layer occupies a distinct frequency range to avoid muddiness.
3. **Volume Balancing** : Adjust the volume of each layer to create a balanced sound.

Practical Layering Examples

1. **Layering a Bass Sound** :

    - **Sub-Bass** : Use a sine wave for the low-end foundation.
    - **Mid-Bass** : Add a saw wave with a low-pass filter for the mid-range punch.
    - **High-Bass** : Use a distorted square wave for added grit and presence.

2. **Layering a Lead Sound** :

    - **Primary Lead** : Start with a bright, detuned saw wave.
    - **Supporting Lead** : Add a slightly different waveform, like a pulse wave, with some modulation.
    - **Harmonics** : Layer a higher octave with subtle effects to add shimmer.

Modulation and Automation

Modulation and automation are powerful tools that add movement and dynamism to your sounds. They involve changing parameters over time, creating evolving and engaging audio.

Modulation

Modulation involves varying a sound parameter using an LFO (Low-Frequency Oscillator), envelope, or other modulation source.

- **LFO** : Use LFOs to modulate parameters like pitch, filter cutoff, and amplitude.
- **Envelopes** : Shape the sound's attack, decay, sustain, and release (ADSR) using envelopes.
- **Automation Clips** : Draw automation clips in FL Studio's playlist to control any parameter over time.

Practical Modulation Examples

1. **Modulating a Filter** :

    - **LFO** : Assign an LFO to the cutoff frequency of a low-pass filter to create a wobble effect.
    - **Envelope** : Use an envelope to create a sweeping filter effect on a lead sound.

2. **Modulating Pitch** :

    - **LFO** : Apply a slow LFO to pitch for a subtle vibrato effect.
    - **Envelope** : Use a pitch envelope to create pitch risers or drops in your sound.

Sound Design for Different Genres

Different genres require different sound design techniques. Understanding the specific requirements of each genre will help you create sounds that fit well within your chosen style.

Electronic Music

Electronic music often relies on synthesized sounds and heavy processing.

- **Basses** : Use FM synthesis and distortion to create aggressive, punchy basses.
- **Leads** : Employ complex modulation and layering to design intricate lead sounds.
- **Pads** : Create lush, evolving pads using additive synthesis and granular effects.

Hip Hop and Trap

Hip hop and trap music require hard-hitting drums and deep basses.

- **Drums** : Sample-based drums with tight, punchy processing. Use EQ and compression to enhance transients.
- **808s** : Design deep, subby basses using sine waves with subtle distortion and pitch modulation.

- **Vocal Chops** : Use sampling and slicing techniques to create rhythmic vocal chops.

Film Scoring and Sound Effects

Film scoring and sound effects require a wide range of sounds to enhance the visual narrative.

- **Atmospheres** : Create immersive soundscapes using field recordings and extensive reverb.
- **Foley** : Record and process real-world sounds to add realism to scenes.
- **Cinematic Hits** : Use layering and heavy processing to design impactful hits and transitions.

Practical Advanced Techniques Examples

1. **Creating a Powerful Bass Sound** :

    - **Layering** : Combine sub-bass, mid-bass, and high-bass layers.
    - **Modulation** : Use an LFO to modulate filter cutoff for a dynamic effect.
    - **Processing** : Apply distortion, EQ, and compression to shape the sound.

2. **Designing a Cinematic Soundscape** :

- **Field Recording** : Capture ambient sounds and layer them for depth.
- **Synthesis** : Add synthesized elements like drones and pads.
- **Effects** : Use reverb, delay, and modulation effects to enhance the atmosphere.

3. **Crafting an Evolving Lead Sound** :

- **Synthesis** : Use a wavetable synth to create the initial sound.
- **Modulation** : Apply envelope modulation to the wavetable position and filter cutoff.
- **Automation** : Automate effects like delay and reverb for added movement.

Tips for Advanced Sound Design

1. **Experiment with Techniques** : Don't be afraid to combine different techniques and effects to discover new sounds.
2. **Use Reference Tracks** : Analyze tracks in your target genre to understand their sound design elements.
3. **Save Your Work** : Save your patches and FX chains as presets for future use and inspiration.
4. **Learn from Others** : Watch tutorials, join forums, and collaborate with other sound designers to expand your knowledge.
5. **Practice Regularly** : Consistent practice is key to mastering advanced sound design techniques.

Conclusion

Advanced sound design techniques like layering, modulation, automation, and genre-specific strategies are essential for creating professional and distinctive sounds. By mastering these techniques and continually experimenting, you'll be able to push the boundaries of your creativity and produce high-quality sound design in FL Studio. As you continue through this book, you'll build on these foundational skills, exploring more advanced techniques and creative possibilities in sound design.

Chapter 6: Practical Sound Design Projects

Introduction

In this chapter, we'll apply the techniques and knowledge you've gained so far to practical sound design projects. These projects are designed to help you develop your skills through hands-on experience. By following these step-by-step guides, you'll create a variety of sounds that you can use in your own music production and sound design work.

Project 1: Creating a Signature Bass Sound

A powerful and distinctive bass sound is essential for many genres of music, particularly electronic and hip-hop. In this project, we'll design a deep, punchy bass sound using Sytrus and Harmor.

Step-by-Step Guide

1. **Initialize Sytrus** :

    - Open Sytrus and select the default patch.
    - Set Operator 1 to a sine wave and lower its octave by one to create a sub-bass foundation.

2. **Add Harmonics with Harmor** :

    - Load Harmor and set the oscillator to a saw wave.
    - Apply a low-pass filter to remove high frequencies, leaving a warm mid-bass.
    - Use unison to add width and detune to create movement.

3. **Layer and Process** :

    - Route both Sytrus and Harmor to a mixer channel.

- Add an EQ to sculpt the frequencies, boosting the low end and cutting unnecessary highs.
- Apply compression to glue the layers together.
- Add a touch of saturation for warmth.

4. **Final Touches** :

- Use a transient shaper to enhance the attack.
- Add a sub-bass enhancer like Fruity Bass Boost if needed.
- Save the patch as a preset for future use.

Project 2: Crafting a Unique Drum Kit

Creating a custom drum kit can give your tracks a unique identity. In this project, we'll assemble a drum kit using FPC and various samples.

Step-by-Step Guide

1. **Gather Samples** :

- Collect drum samples from your library or record your own.
- Ensure you have a variety of kicks, snares, hats, and percussion sounds.

2. **Load Samples into FPC** :

- Open FPC and import your samples into different pads.
- Assign kicks to the lower pads, snares to the middle, and hats/percussion to the upper pads.

3. **Layer and Process** :

    - For each drum hit, layer multiple samples to add depth. For example, layer a punchy kick with a sub-kick.
    - Use EQ to carve out frequencies and prevent muddiness.
    - Apply compression to tighten the sounds.

4. **Add Effects** :

    - Add reverb to snares and claps for space.
    - Use transient shaping to enhance the attack of kicks and snares.
    - Apply subtle distortion to hats for grit.

5. **Save Your Kit** :

    - Save your custom drum kit as an FPC preset for easy access.

Project 3: Designing a Cinematic Soundscape

Cinematic soundscapes are essential for film scoring, video games, and ambient music. In this project, we'll create an immersive soundscape using field recordings and synthesis.

Step-by-Step Guide

1. **Capture Field Recordings** :

    - Use a portable recorder to capture environmental sounds (e.g., forest, cityscape).
    - Import the recordings into FL Studio.

2. **Edit and Layer Recordings** :

    - Open Edison and edit the recordings, removing unwanted noise.
    - Layer different recordings to create a rich texture.

3. **Add Synthesized Elements** :

    - Use Sytrus to create a drone sound. Start with a sine wave and add subtle modulation.
    - Use Harmor to create evolving pads. Apply slow-moving filters and modulation for depth.

4. **Apply Effects** :

    - Use reverb and delay to add space and depth to your soundscape.
    - Add EQ to shape the overall sound, ensuring each element has its own space.

5. **Automation and Final Touches** :

    - Automate volume, panning, and effects to add movement.
    - Export the final soundscape as a high-quality audio file.

Project 4: Building an Evolving Lead Sound

An evolving lead sound can add excitement and interest to your tracks. In this project, we'll create a dynamic lead using Serum and FL Studio's automation features.

Step-by-Step Guide

1. **Initialize Serum** :

    - Open Serum and load a basic saw wave.
    - Set the oscillator to a unison mode with slight detune for a fuller sound.

2. **Modulate the Sound** :

    - Assign an LFO to the wavetable position for a morphing effect.
    - Use an envelope to control the filter cutoff, creating a sweeping effect.

3. **Add Effects** :

    - Apply distortion and chorus to add character.
    - Use reverb and delay to create space and movement.

4. **Automate Parameters** :

    - Draw automation clips in the playlist for parameters like filter cutoff, wavetable position, and effects mix.
    - Experiment with different automation shapes to create evolving patterns.

5. **Final Touches** :

    - Add EQ and compression to polish the sound.
    - Save the preset for future use.

Project 5: Crafting a Glitch Effect

Glitch effects add a unique, digital character to your sounds. In this project, we'll create a glitchy, stuttering effect using Gross Beat and Slicex.

Step-by-Step Guide

1. **Prepare the Source Material** :

    - Choose a sample or loop to apply the glitch effect to.
    - Import the sample into the playlist.

2. **Slice and Rearrange with Slicex** :

    - Open Slicex and import the sample.
    - Adjust slice points to chop the sample into smaller segments.
    - Rearrange the slices to create a stuttering pattern.

3. **Apply Gross Beat** :

    - Load Gross Beat onto the channel with the sample.
    - Choose a preset from the Glitch or Stutter categories.
    - Adjust the grid to create rhythmic glitch patterns.

4. **Add Effects** :

    - Apply reverb and delay to smooth out the transitions.
    - Use EQ to shape the glitch effect, enhancing certain frequencies.

5. **Automation and Final Touches** :

    - Automate Gross Beat parameters for dynamic glitch effects.
    - Export the final glitch effect for use in your projects.

Tips for Successful Sound Design Projects

1. **Plan Ahead** : Have a clear idea of the sound you want to create before you start.
2. **Experiment Freely** : Don't be afraid to try unconventional techniques and settings.
3. **Take Breaks** : Give your ears a rest to maintain objectivity and avoid ear fatigue.
4. **Collaborate and Learn** : Share your projects with others and learn from their feedback and techniques.
5. **Document Your Process** : Keep notes on your sound design process for future reference and to help replicate successful techniques.

Conclusion

These practical sound design projects are designed to help you apply the techniques and knowledge you've gained throughout this book. By working through these projects, you'll develop a deeper understanding of sound design and build a collection of unique sounds that you can use in your music and audio productions. Keep experimenting, practicing, and pushing the boundaries of your creativity. As you continue through this book, you'll explore even more advanced techniques and creative possibilities in sound design.

Chapter 7: Troubleshooting and Tips

Introduction

Sound design can be a complex and sometimes frustrating process. Issues like muddy mixes, weak sounds, or harsh frequencies can hinder your progress. In this chapter, we'll explore common sound design problems and provide practical solutions. We'll also share workflow tips to help you stay organized and efficient, as well as creative tips to keep your inspiration flowing.

Common Sound Design Issues

Muddy Mixes

A muddy mix lacks clarity and definition, making it difficult to distinguish between different elements.
Solutions:

1. **EQ Cleanup** :

   - Use a high-pass filter to remove unnecessary low frequencies from non-bass elements.
   - Identify and reduce overlapping frequencies between instruments using a parametric EQ.

2. **Panning** :

   - Spread elements across the stereo field to create separation.
   - Pan supporting elements slightly left or right to give the main elements more space.

3. **Layering and Frequency Slotting** :

   - Ensure each layer occupies its own frequency range.
   - Avoid overloading the same frequency range with multiple elements.

Weak Sounds

Weak sounds lack impact and presence, often getting lost in the mix.
Solutions:

1. **Layering** :

    - Layer multiple sounds to add depth and richness.
    - Combine different sound sources to create a fuller sound.

2. **Compression** :

    - Use compression to add punch and control dynamics.
    - Apply parallel compression to retain the natural dynamics while adding strength.

3. **Saturation and Distortion** :

    - Add subtle saturation to enhance harmonics and presence.
    - Use distortion creatively to add grit and character.

Harsh Frequencies

Harsh frequencies can cause listener fatigue and make a mix sound unpleasant.
Solutions:

1. **EQ Notching** :

    - Identify and reduce harsh frequencies using a narrow EQ notch.
    - Use a spectrum analyzer to pinpoint problematic frequencies.

2. **Dynamic EQ** :

    - Apply dynamic EQ to control harsh frequencies only when they become problematic.
    - Use multiband compression to tame specific frequency ranges.

3. **De-essing** :

    - Use a de-esser to reduce harsh sibilance in vocals and high-frequency content.
    - Adjust the threshold and frequency range to target specific problem areas.

Workflow Tips

Organizing Your Project

Keeping your FL Studio projects organized can save you time and reduce frustration.

1. **Label and Color Code** :

    - Label all tracks, mixer channels, and patterns clearly.
    - Use color coding to visually distinguish different elements.

2. **Use Folders and Groups** :

    - Group related tracks together using track groups and folders.
    - Collapse groups when not in use to keep your project tidy.

3. **Template Projects** :

    - Create template projects with your preferred setup, including commonly used tracks and plugins.
    - Use templates as a starting point for new projects to save time.

Efficient Sound Design

Efficiency is key to maintaining creativity and productivity.

1. **Preset Libraries** :

    - Build a library of your favorite presets and patches for quick access.
    - Categorize presets by type and use tags for easy searching.

2. **Macro Controls** :

    - Use macro controls to simplify complex sound design processes.
    - Assign multiple parameters to a single macro knob for quick adjustments.

3. **Keyboard Shortcuts** :

    - Learn and use keyboard shortcuts to speed up your workflow.
    - Customize shortcuts to suit your preferences and workflow.

Backup and Version Control

Protect your work by regularly backing up your projects and using version control.

1. **Regular Backups** :

    - Save multiple versions of your project as you work.
    - Use cloud storage or an external drive for additional backups.

2. **Version Control** :

    - Use a version control system like Git to track changes and revert to previous versions if needed.
    - Comment on changes to keep track of your progress and decisions.

Creative Tips

Breaking Creative Blocks

Creative blocks are a common challenge for sound designers. Here are some strategies to overcome them:

1. **Change Your Environment** :

    - Work in a different location or rearrange your workspace.
    - Take breaks and get fresh air to reset your mind.

2. **Set Limitations** :

    - Challenge yourself by setting limitations, such as using only one synth or a specific set of samples.
    - Limitations can spark creativity and force you to think outside the box.

3. **Collaborate with Others** :

    - Work with other musicians and sound designers to gain new perspectives and ideas.
    - Share projects and feedback to inspire each other.

Experimentation

Experimentation is crucial for discovering new sounds and techniques.

1. **Try Unconventional Techniques** :

- Use effects in unexpected ways, such as applying reverb before distortion.
- Experiment with extreme settings to see how they affect your sound.

2. **Layer Unlikely Sounds** :

- Combine sounds that you wouldn't normally layer together.
- Use field recordings or found sounds as layers to add uniqueness.

3. **Reverse Engineering** :

- Analyze and recreate sounds from your favorite tracks.
- Dissect presets and patches to understand how they are constructed.

Collaborating with Others

Collaboration can open up new creative possibilities and help you grow as a sound designer.

1. **Share Projects** :

- Share your FL Studio projects with collaborators to get feedback and new ideas.

- Use project files and stems for seamless collaboration.

2. **Learn from Peers** :

    - Join online communities and forums to connect with other sound designers.
    - Participate in challenges and collaborations to expand your skills.

3. **Respect Creative Differences** :

    - Embrace different perspectives and ideas.
    - Communicate openly and constructively with collaborators.

Conclusion

Troubleshooting common sound design issues and implementing effective workflow and creative strategies can significantly enhance your sound design process. By staying organized, experimenting freely, and collaborating with others, you'll overcome obstacles and continue to grow as a sound designer. As you progress through this book, keep these tips in mind to refine your skills and maintain your creative momentum.

Conclusion

The Journey of Sound Design Mastery

Congratulations on reaching the end of "Sound Design Mastery with FL Studio: Crafting Professional Sounds." This book has taken you on a comprehensive journey through the world of sound design, from foundational concepts to advanced techniques. You've learned to harness the power of FL Studio's built-in plugins and third-party VSTs, explored various synthesis and sampling methods, and developed skills in creating intricate FX chains. Along the way, you've tackled practical projects and gained insights into troubleshooting common issues and optimizing your workflow.

Key Takeaways

1. **Foundational Knowledge** : Understanding the basics of sound design, including synthesis, sampling, and effects processing, is crucial. Mastering these fundamentals provides a solid foundation for more advanced techniques.
2. **Synthesis Techniques** : You've explored various types of synthesis—subtractive, FM, additive, wavetable, and granular—and learned how to use FL Studio's synthesizers, such as Sytrus, Harmor, and 3xOSC, to create a wide range of sounds.
3. **Sampling Strategies** : Effective sampling involves capturing, editing, and manipulating audio. Tools like Edison, DirectWave, FPC, and Slicex in FL Studio allow

you to creatively transform raw audio into unique sound elements.
4. **FX Chain Exploration** : Building and experimenting with FX chains is essential for shaping and enhancing sounds. Understanding how to use EQ, compression, reverb, delay, distortion, and other effects helps you craft professional-quality audio.
5. **Advanced Techniques** : Layering, modulation, and automation are powerful techniques that add depth and movement to your sounds. Additionally, genre-specific sound design strategies enable you to tailor your sounds to fit various musical contexts.
6. **Practical Projects** : Hands-on projects are invaluable for applying your knowledge and developing your skills. Creating signature bass sounds, custom drum kits, cinematic soundscapes, evolving lead sounds, and glitch effects allows you to put theory into practice.
7. **Troubleshooting and Tips** : Addressing common sound design issues, optimizing your workflow, and employing creative strategies ensure that you remain productive and inspired. Overcoming challenges and experimenting with new ideas are key to growth as a sound designer.

The Path Forward

Sound design is a continuously evolving field. The skills and knowledge you've gained from this book are just the beginning. Here are some steps to continue your journey:

1. **Keep Practicing** : Consistent practice is essential. Regularly experiment with new sounds, techniques, and tools to expand your skill set.

2. **Stay Updated** : The world of sound design and music production is always advancing. Stay informed about new plugins, software updates, and industry trends.
3. **Learn from Others** : Join online communities, attend workshops, and collaborate with other sound designers. Sharing knowledge and experiences helps you grow and stay inspired.
4. **Create and Share** : Apply your skills to real-world projects. Whether you're producing music, designing sounds for films or games, or creating audio for other media, put your knowledge to use. Share your work with the world to receive feedback and recognition.
5. **Stay Curious** : Never stop exploring. Sound design is an art form that thrives on curiosity and innovation. Embrace new challenges and push the boundaries of what's possible.

Final Thoughts

Sound design is a blend of technical skill and creative intuition. With the tools and techniques covered in this book, you have the foundation to create professional and distinctive sounds. Remember that sound design is not just about the final product but also about the process. Enjoy the journey, embrace experimentation, and let your creativity soar.
Thank you for embarking on this sound design adventure with "Sound Design Mastery with FL Studio: Crafting Professional Sounds." Now, go forth and create something extraordinary!

Index

A

- Additive Synthesis, 6, 7, 8, 9
- Advanced Sound Design Techniques, 33-37
- Automation, 33, 35, 36

B

- Basic Sound Design Projects, 25-32
- Built-In Effects, 17, 18, 19, 20
- Built-In Synthesizers, 7, 8, 9

C

- Compression, 19, 22, 35
- Creative Sampling, 15, 16
- Creative Tips, 41-42

D

- Delay, 20, 21, 30, 31, 36
- DirectWave, 12, 13, 26, 27

- Distortion, 21, 22

E

- Edison, 12, 13, 26, 27
- Equalization (EQ), 17, 19, 22, 26, 35
- Experimentation, 42

F

- FabFilter Pro-Q 3, 22
- Field Recording, 15, 16, 29, 30
- FPC (Fruity Pad Controller), 13, 14, 27, 28
- Fruity Delay 3, 20
- Fruity Fast Dist, 21
- Fruity Limiter, 19
- Fruity Reeverb 2, 18

G

- Granular Synthesis, 9, 10, 11

H

- Harmor, 8, 9, 11, 26
- Harsh Frequencies, 38

I

- Introduction to Sound Design, 4-6
- Issues in Sound Design, 37-39

K

- Key Takeaways, 44

L

- Layering, 33, 34, 35
- LFO (Low-Frequency Oscillator), 34

M

- Massive (Native Instruments), 10, 11

- Mid/Side Processing, 19
- Modulation, 34, 36, 42
- Muddy Mixes, 37, 38

O

- Omnisphere (Spectrasonics), 10, 11
- Organizing Your Project, 39, 40

P

- Parametric EQ 2, 17
- Parallel Processing, 23, 24
- Practical Sound Design Projects, 25-32
- Project 1: Creating a Signature Bass Sound, 25, 26
- Project 2: Crafting a Unique Drum Kit, 27, 28
- Project 3: Designing a Cinematic Soundscape, 29, 30
- Project 4: Building an Evolving Lead Sound, 31, 32
- Project 5: Crafting a Glitch Effect, 32
- Poizone, 9, 10
- Preset Libraries, 40

R

- Reverb, 18, 21, 30, 31
- Resampling, 15, 16
- Reverb (Valhalla Room), 22

S

- Sampling Strategies, 12-16
- Serum (Xfer Records), 10, 11
- Signal Processing, 17, 23, 24
- Slicing (Slicex), 14, 15, 32
- Sound Design for Different Genres, 35, 36
- Subtractive Synthesis, 6, 7, 8, 9
- Sytrus, 7, 8, 26, 30

T

- Third-Party VST Effects, 22
- Third-Party VST Synthesizers, 10, 11
- Toxic Biohazard, 9, 10
- Troubleshooting, 37-39

U

- Unison, 8, 9, 31

V

- Valhalla Room, 22
- Version Control, 40
- Vocal Chops, 36

W

- Wavetable Synthesis, 9, 10, 11
- Weak Sounds, 38

Z

- Zoning (DirectWave), 13, 14

Made in United States
North Haven, CT
11 November 2024